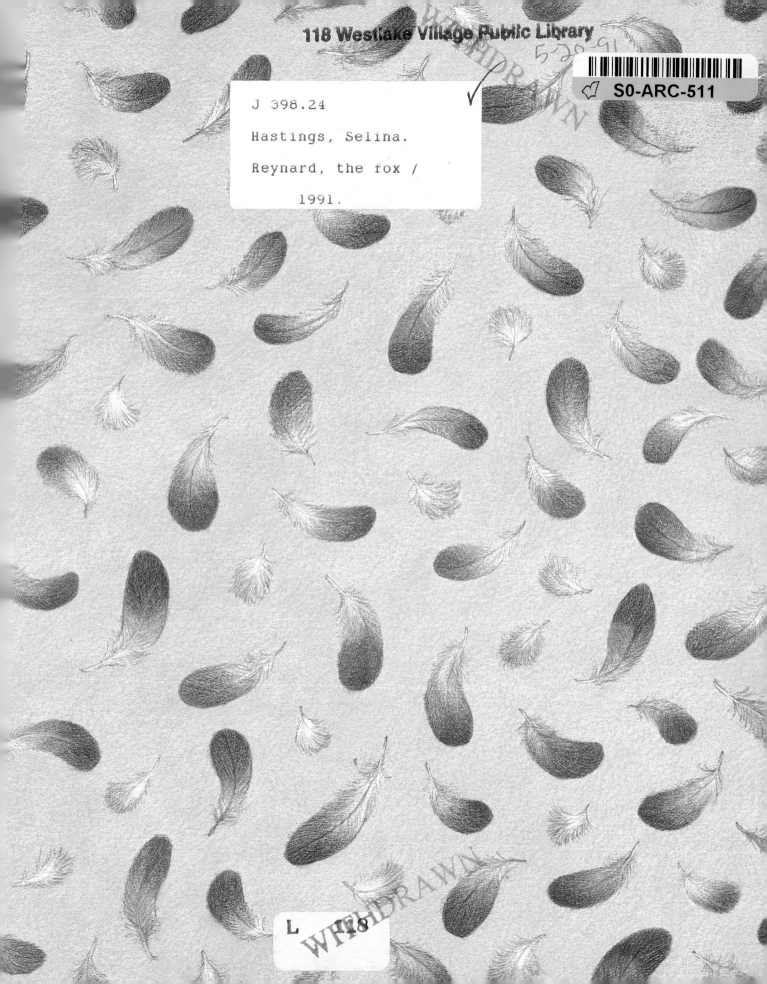

For Joe
S.H.

Library of Congress Cataloging in Publication Data
Hastings, Selina. Reynard the fox / retold by Selina Hastings ;
pictures by Graham Percy.   p. cm.
Summary: A retelling of the various adventures and
schemes of the lying, cheating, and cowardly Reynard.
1. Reynard the Fox (Legendary character)
[1. Reynard the Fox (Legendary character)
2. Fables.   3. Foxes—Folklore.]   I. Percy, Graham, ill.   II. Title.
PZ8.2.H28Re   1991   398.24'52974442—dc20   90-11105 CIP AC
ISBN 0-688-09949-1 (trade)—ISBN 0-688-10156-9 (lib)
Printed in Hong Kong by South China Printing Co. (1988) Ltd.
First U.S. edition 1991
1   3   5   7   9   10   8   6   4   2

Reynard the Fox

retold by Selina Hastings

illustrated by Graham Percy

TAMBOURINE BOOKS

New York

INTRODUCTION

Stories in which animals talk and act like people have an ancient history, and have existed for thousands of years all over the world. This particular story, of Reynard the cunning Fox who always outwits the other members of the animal kingdom, probably descends from Roman times, from Æsop's "Fable of the Sick Lion." The tale of Reynard was particularly popular in Northern Europe during the Middle Ages; he even appeared on the walls of Strasbourg Cathedral in two pictures on either side of the pulpit, one showing the Fox playing his fiddle, the other the Fox playing dead at his own funeral.

In all these stories the plot depends on the principal that brute strength is inferior to wisdom. We know that the Fox, however wicked and greedy, will always get the better of the Lion, however noble, and of the Wolf, however brave – although it should perhaps be mentioned that the Fox's opponents are by no means always noble, nor are they always brave. In some ways this animal world can be seen as a satirical reflection of our world, the world of people; but although the beasts' behavior is very human, they never abandon their animal natures. Reynard, walking upright, talking, and thinking like a person, is still by nature a fox, just as Bruin remains bearlike, Tibert catlike, and so on.

Although fragments of the Reynard stories were known in England from a much earlier date, it was not until 1481 that a complete translation was made from the Dutch by William Caxton, famous as the first man to print a book in English. This present retelling is based on Caxton's version, although of course in a very much shortened form. However, the basic plot remains unaltered, as do the animal characters in all their kindness, cruelty, trickiness, and charm.

Reynard

Selina Hastings

The shadow of Reynard the Fox had fallen across the lives of all the animals. It was a lithe, narrow shadow, a shadow that moved fast and dangerously. No one had escaped without some injury to himself, to his family or friends. By now the animals were angry, and so frightened of Reynard that they came in a body to see the Lion, King of the Beasts, and demand that this most slippery of all his subjects be brought to justice.

The first to come forward was Reynard's old enemy, Isegrim the Wolf. "My lord King," he began, "for many years I, my wife, and family have suffered the most terrible injuries from this cunning and malicious animal. Only last week he broke into my house and attacked my two children as they lay innocently asleep. I implore Your Majesty to protect us all and rid us of this Fox!"

Next Curtois, the little Dog, took the floor, tail between his legs, ears flat against his head. "Sire," he whined, "on the coldest night of last winter when I lay chained to my kennel with nothing to eat but a small slice of pudding, Reynard came creeping up and stole my pudding!"

And so the complaints continued, each animal telling his story, all of them pointing to the Fox as thief and murderer.

When they had done, Reynard's nephew, Grimbard the Badger, called for silence, loyally determined to make a case in defense of his Uncle. "These stories are all very well, but there are two sides to any argument. For instance, Isegrim, as we know, time and time again has himself attacked and cheated Reynard. And as for Curtois, he stole the pudding, and who can blame Reynard for taking stolen goods from a thief?

"And whatever he may have done in the past," Grimbard went on, "my Uncle tells me that he is now a reformed character: He lives very simply, never eats meat, has given away all his wealth, and spends hours a day on his knees in penance for his sins. In fact I hear he has grown quite pale and thin with all his prayer and fasting."

No sooner were these words said than into the hall
flapped Chanticleer the Cock. He was beating his feathered
breast, weeping over the corpse of his daughter Copple,
carried in on a bier by two of her sisters. The head of this
unfortunate hen that very day had been bitten off by
Reynard.

"My lord King, I demand justice! By lies and trickery
that wicked Fox has murdered eleven of my fifteen
children, of whom Copple was the youngest, the last to
hatch from the egg. Now I have only four left: Must they,
too, be victims of this criminal?"

At this the royal Lion rose to his feet. "I have heard enough," he declared. "Sir Chanticleer, I offer you my deepest sympathy and promise that your daughter shall be buried with full honors. And as for Reynard, I hereby

issue a command that he immediately appear before this court to answer the charges made against him!"

The King then summoned Bruin the Bear to carry this message to the Fox.

When Bruin, full of confidence, lumbered up to Castle Malepardus where Reynard lived, he found the drawbridge raised against him. As no one answered his knock, he sat back on his haunches and loudly called out the King's summons. "And if you fail to appear," he boomed triumphantly, "your life shall be forfeit!"

Inside the castle, high along the battlements, the Fox lay listening and smiling to himself. When the Bear had finished speaking Reynard quietly slunk off to one of the deeply-dug holes of which there are many in Malepardus and there he plotted what to do. Then after a short while he sauntered out to greet Bruin.

"Please forgive me for being so slow to welcome you,"
he said politely, "but I was at my prayers. I am sorry, too,
that you have come all this way for nothing: Tomorrow
I would have gone to court of my own accord. And I am
afraid you will find the journey back tediously slow as I
am weak from fasting, having eaten nothing these last days
but a little honeycomb."

Bruin threw back his great stupid head. "Honeycomb!" he bellowed. "I love honeycomb! Give me one taste of honeycomb and I will be your friend for life!"

"Nothing easier," said Reynard pleasantly. And he led the Bear to the house of a local forester in whose yard lay a recently felled oak; its trunk had been partially split, the sides held apart by wedges.

Reynard pointed to the tree. "In there, my dear Bruin, you will find more honeycomb than even you can eat in a year."

Licking his lips, the greedy Bear padded eagerly to the fallen tree and pushed his head deep down into the cleft. At which exact moment the Fox pulled out the wedges and Bruin was trapped.

His roars of pain and panic brought the woodsman
running from his house, soon followed by the whole
village, who set upon the miserable Bear with sticks and
cudgels, until with a gigantic effort, he wrenched free
and galloped off towards the river.

There he plunged into the water to soothe his many cuts and bruises, to the entertainment of Reynard who lay concealed and at a safe distance along the bank.

Eventually, aching and ashamed, Bruin arrived back at court. The King was very angry when he saw the state his messenger was in. Determined that the Fox should be made to answer his summons, he called Tibert the Cat to go in the Bear's place and bring Reynard before him.

Tibert made his way to Malepardus with a sinking heart. Small and easily made nervous, the Cat had little faith that he would be successful where the big and forceful Bear had failed. As he drew near the castle, he saw Reynard leaning out from above the entrance, watching his approach. Swallowing hard, Tibert took a deep breath. "Reynard, I have been ordered to bring this message from the King: If you do not at once answer his summons and come back with me to court, not only will you face death, but all your lands and property will be confiscated!"

Reynard smiled. "Nothing would give me greater
pleasure than to return with you this instant; but it is
already growing dark and you must be hungry. Stay here
tonight, and we will leave at dawn tomorrow."

The Cat, tired by his journey and reassured by Reynard's
friendly manner, agreed and allowed himself to be led
inside. "Now," said Reynard, "what may I offer you to
eat? I have a very nice honeycomb."

"Honeycomb!" Tibert exclaimed in distaste. "That is not, I must confess, a food I care for. Have you no mice?"

"Why, certainly, nothing could be easier. The priest in the village has a barn so full of mice he is at his wits' end what to do."

"Take me there," said Tibert, his whiskers quivering, "and I will be your friend for life."

Now it so happened that the previous night Reynard, creeping through a hole well known to himself in the side of the barn, had stolen one of the priest's fattest hens, and he knew that the priest would set a trap for him, as he had often done before. He led Tibert to the barn and pointed to the hole. "Jump in through there, and when you have eaten all you want, I will escort you home where my wife will be expecting us."

Although his mouth was watering, Tibert hesitated. "But is it safe?" he whispered nervously.

"Tibert, surely you are not afraid? This is something I have done many times myself, and would do oftener if I had more of an appetite for mice."

So Tibert sprang through the hole and straight into the trap.

His yowls of anguish soon woke the priest who, believing he had caught the Fox at last, leapt out of bed and running into the barn started beating Tibert with a heavy stick. The Cat, desperate for his life, bit the priest so hard on the hand that the man momentarily lost consciousness, which just gave Tibert time to gnaw through the snare and escape.

When the next day Tibert, bruised and bedraggled, limped into court the King was angrier than ever. This time he sent for Grimbard the Badger, and instructed him carefully. "Grimbard, I know you have influence with your Uncle. I want you to tell him that I am most displeased, and that if he again fails to obey my summons then he will be judged guilty by his absence and condemned to death!"

When the Badger arrived at Malepardus he found
Reynard and his wife Ermelin inside a walled garden
playing a game of feathers with their two small children.

But Grimbard, conscious of the seriousness of his mission, ignored this pretty scene and began at once. "Uncle, you must listen to what I am about to say. If again you disregard the King's command, then your life will be forfeit, your castle destroyed, and your entire family taken into slavery."

"My dear nephew," Reynard smoothly replied. "Please do not distress yourself. Of course I will do as you wish. I have many enemies at court who slander me; but I have nothing to fear. The King is wise and just, and I do not hesitate to put myself in his hands."

Early next morning they set out. Reynard took a most loving leave of his wife, who burst into tears, and the two cubs howled to see their father go.

As they trudged along the road together, Grimbard, who had an honest, simple nature, tried hard to make Reynard see the error of his ways. "You would be so much happier, Uncle," he said earnestly, "if you would only learn to love your neighbor and live by the law of the land."

Reynard sighed and did his best to look ashamed. "Yes, Grimbard, you are right. I have been guilty of much wickedness. I promise you, however, that it is all in the past. I truly repent of what I have done, and from this day on I shall devote myself to penance and good works." He sighed again.

A little way further on they passed a convent by the side of the road, in front of which, on a small green, some geese and hens were feeding. Suddenly and without warning Reynard pounced on a fat pullet, catching it by the tail. But the fowl, squawking furiously, struggled free, leaving him with only a mouthful of feathers. "Oh, Uncle," said Grimbard, his small face furrowed with reproach, "will you sacrifice all your good intentions already, and for only a bit of chicken?"

Reynard looked embarrassed. "I forgot myself just then; I assure you it will not happen again." But still his eyes remained on the poultry.

"Why do you go on looking at those birds?" Grimbard asked.

"Because," replied Reynard with barely the suspicion of a smile, "because I am praying for the souls of all the geese and hens I have eaten over the years."

"Hmm," said Grimbard.

When Reynard and Grimbard were seen approaching the town the animals jostled and pushed each other in their turns to be the first in court, eager to witness the downfall of the hated Fox. Reynard swaggered bravely as he strode up the street, but in his heart he was afraid for he knew only too well that the charges he would have to answer were many and serious.

At last he stood before the Lion King. "Your Majesty," he said bowing low, "you see in front of you the truest and most loyal of all your subjects. I am Your Highness's devoted servant, yours to command, wishing only to serve you to the very best of my humble ability."

"That's enough of that, Reynard," interrupted the King impatiently. "I want to hear no more of your flowery and flattering speeches. Now the time has come for you to face your accusers and defend yourself as best you can."

At these words the animals surged forward, each one
clamoring to put his case, all determined to have
vengeance on their common enemy. The King saw that
the feeling against Reynard was so strong that an orderly
trial would be impossible; clearly the evidence against the
Fox was overwhelming. And so, calling for silence, he
declared that Reynard be judged guilty and condemned
to death.

A shiver of excitement went through the crowd; but in Reynard's veins the blood ran cold: Had the time come at last for him to die?

Bruin and Isegrim, hardly able to conceal their delight,

stepped forward, one on each side of the Fox, to lead him to the gallows. Tibert, carrying the noose, fell in behind, and after him the King and Queen, and after them the other animals.

When this gloating procession reached the foot of the scaffold just outside the walls of the town, Reynard, who all the while had been thinking hard, turned to face the Lion. "My lord, as I am about to die, I implore you to let me make my confession so that I can leave this life with a clear conscience."

The Lion nodded his assent. "I have been guilty of many things," Reynard began, his voice like honey, his yellow eyes gleaming with insincerity, "but nothing do I regret so much as having been the cause of distress to Your Majesty and to my fellow creatures. I most bitterly repent the evil I have done and indeed, to have a second chance of leading a good life, I would surrender all my earthly riches, great as they are."

At the word "riches" the King pricked up his ears. "What riches are these, Reynard?"

"Sire, I am ashamed to say the treasure I speak of was not honestly acquired. It is treasure I stole, but stole in order to secure both Your Majesty's life and the safety of your Kingdom.

"It happened like this: Two years ago my father, a fox of immense cunning and ambition, came across a hoard of buried treasure. With it he planned to raise an army, depose Your Majesty, and himself seize the throne. Fortunately I discovered both the treasure and his treacherous plot. When I confronted him, my father, overcome by guilt and frustration, hanged himself.

"Just as you, Sire, are about to hang me, the most faithful of your subjects."

Said the King, who was stirred by this story, and stirred even more by a desire to get possession of the treasure, "I am touched by your words, Reynard, and I intend to give you your second chance. If you will tell me where I may find this rich hoard, I will grant you an absolute pardon."

Reynard promised that he would do at once what the Lion asked, and he smiled to himself as well he might, for life suddenly was sweet. The animals stood appalled as the King gestured to Reynard's guards, Bruin and Isegrim, to let their prisoner stand free. "And you must come with us," said the genial King, "to help us dig."

For a moment Reynard felt a tremor of panic; but quickly recovering himself he replied, "My liege, I cannot. Now my life has been restored I must make my confession in church. Until I have done that I am not worthy to be in your company."

Then the Fox leapt from the scaffold and, running belly to the ground, swiftly made his escape.

The foolish Lion then gravely addressed his subjects. The Fox, he said, despite the record of his past, was one of the most noble of animals, a loyal subject whose good nature has been most sadly misunderstood. "The name of Reynard – Sir Reynard from this day on – be honored by you all. He and his wife and children must henceforward be treated with the greatest deference and respect."

Now for some this was asking too much, that the bushy-tailed scoundrel should not only get away with his life but be praised by the King for his stainless character! Bruin, Isegrim, and Tibert were outraged. "I'll tell the King," said Isegrim, shrill with fury. "I'll tell him what to do with his noble Fox!"

"I, too," said Bruin. "I'd sooner drink poison than be polite to that rascal!" And the two of them began to push forward through the crowd.

Tibert, however, stayed where he was and said nothing; a cat of timorous disposition, he was too anxious for the safety of his skin to risk upsetting so dangerous an enemy as the Fox.

The Wolf and Bear, however, were made of stronger stuff. Which perhaps was fortunate, for as soon as the King heard what they were saying he ordered their arrest and had them thrown into prison for treason.

To celebrate the honoring of Reynard and to mark the beginning of a new period of peace and harmony in the animal kingdom, the Lion gave a feast to which all his subjects were invited. Almost all his subjects—no invitation reached the Wolf and the Bear in their prison cell and the Fox, for reasons of his own, was mysteriously absent. The rest, however, enjoyed themselves eating and drinking as though famine were only just round the corner.

When the banquet was no more than half eaten, into the hall, limping, came Laprell the Rabbit. Throwing himself at the King's feet he panted out the following story: Less than an hour ago ... on his way home past Malepardus ... Reynard sitting outside the gate ... nodded civilly to each other... And then as Laprell passed, the Fox shot out his foot, tripped up Laprell and sent him flying. It was nothing short of a miracle, gasped the Rabbit, that he had survived with his life and was here to tell the tale.

No sooner had he finished speaking than the Rook
Corbaut flapped in in a state of deep distress: He and his
wife Sharpbeak had been peacefully feeding on the
common when they noticed Reynard lying apparently
lifeless on the ground. Full of concern the kindly
Sharpbeak went hopping over to see what she could do.
As she put her ear to the Fox's heart, Reynard opened
his mouth and bit off her head!

When he heard this, the Lion King, realizing he had been tricked yet again, lost all hold on both his patience and his temper. Stopping only to order the immediate release from prison of the Wolf and Bear, he swore that he would raise an army and himself lay siege to Malepardus and rid the world forever of Reynard and his family.

These stern words were greeted with approval by the animals – except for Grimbard who, loyal to the last, could not help but feel sorry for his disreputable Uncle. Without anyone noticing, he slipped quietly away and ran as fast as he could to Malepardus.

Here he found Reynard in a cheerful mood, observing with interest a pair of newly fledged pigeons balanced on their nest and about to try their wings. He welcomed Grimbard and said what a pleasant surprise it was to see his nephew again so soon.

"Oh, Uncle, you are in great danger," Grimbard began, anxiously wringing his paws, and told him what the King was planning.

"Oh, don't let us bother about that," Reynard lightly replied. "No one is going to get the better of me. Tomorrow I will go with you to the court to talk to the King.

"Now come inside and let's enjoy ourselves. All I ask is that you say nothing of this to my wife, for she is inclined to worry."

And the two of them went into the castle and sat down to a substantial dinner served to them by Ermelin.

After they had eaten Reynard took Grimbard to see his children, Rossel and Reynardine, who were playing with some baby chicks. "How do you like my two young cubs?" asked Reynard, proudly patting their glossy heads.

"You can see how they take after their father. They have learned their lesson well. Already they know how to pick a victim, how to deceive him with flattery, then to move in for the kill with a smile."

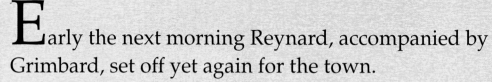

Early the next morning Reynard, accompanied by Grimbard, set off yet again for the town.

Once more Reynard stood before the King. In spite of the carelessness of his manner, the Fox had passed an uneasy night. He loved the excitement of the chase but now his pursuers were alarmingly close, and a disagreeable end was only too clearly in sight. Reynard knelt humbly in front of the Lion.

This time, however, the Lion was not to be moved.
"Reynard, prepare yourself for execution. You have
proved yourself as false to me as you were to the Rabbit
and the Rook, the story of whose wicked treatment at
your hands has just come to my ears."

It was now that Reynard saw his chance. "Sire, those
two are old enemies of mine and both of them have
slandered me. If I were guilty, would I be here now? My
conscience is clear. But if Laprell or Corbaut or anyone
else wishes to accuse me, then let them challenge me to
fight, and by this means I will prove my innocence!"

The assembled beasts were amazed at his cheek. How dare Reynard speak with such conviction of his innocence! Several heads turned expectantly towards the Rabbit and the Rook, but Laprell and Corbaut, knowing only too well Reynard's reputation as a fighter, had no wish to take him on and both slunk timidly away. For some minutes there was silence.

Then Isegrim, furious at Reynard's ploy, stepped forward. "I challenge you, Reynard. I know you for what you are – a thief, a liar and a murderer! Let us fight and see who comes out best!"

Several in the crowd applauded, before being quieted by the King. "I hereby declare," he said, "that Reynard and Isegrim shall meet tomorrow in single combat, the outcome to decide once and forever the guilt or innocence of the Fox!"

Reynard had always taken pleasure in a good skirmish and not since he was a cub had he been beaten. But Isegrim was bigger and stronger than he, and Reynard knew that he would need every trick in the book to defeat him. He went to his Aunt, the Ape Dame Rukenaw, who was fond of him and whom he knew to be wise. She clipped his pelt and covered him thickly in oil.

"Remember," she said, "keep your tail between your legs, and then there is no way that the Wolf will be able to catch hold of you."

Reynard thanked her for her help, and then trotted off, quite calm, to wait for what the next day would bring.

He lay down in the long grass under a tree and slept soundly until sunrise when an amiable young cousin, an otter, brought him a fat duckling to eat. Having made a leisurely breakfast, Reynard strolled over to the place appointed for the fight.

Here a small square had been roped off. Isegrim had
already arrived, and was boasting loudly to his supporters,
of whom there were many, that now at last the shameless
Fox would receive the punishment he deserved. The
King and Queen were present, and all the courtiers; flags
fluttered in the breeze; a band played martial music.

No one had come to cheer on Reynard except his Aunt Rukenaw and the faithful Grimbard.

The Leopard had been appointed to act as umpire, and he it was who called the two opponents into the ring.

As soon as the signal was given, Isegrim went for
Reynard with all the pent-up fury of the hatred of a
lifetime, ears back, jaws snapping, eyes red with rage.
But Reynard was light on his feet and nimble, and
with his oiled skin as slithery as a snake.

Each time the Wolf tried to catch him in his teeth, Reynard twisted out of his way, scuffing the dust in Isegrim's face, nipping at his legs, and tiring the bigger, heavier animal with the suddenness of his movements. Several times the two of them rolled over on the ground together, tearing at each other with their claws, but on each occasion the well-oiled Fox slid out from under his opponent and away to the far side of the ring.

Then at last, while Isegrim paused panting for breath, Reynard came up behind him and hit him so hard on the back of the neck that the Wolf collapsed unconscious on the ground.

The Leopard declared the fight over, and the Lion King rose from his seat to announce the winner. "Sir Reynard, the victory is yours. By this contest you have proved yourself innocent. Let me embrace you. From this day you and your family will be honored as the highest in the land, and never again will I nor anyone doubt your word or deed!"

When the animals saw how Reynard was restored to favor, with the King publicly embracing him, it was remarkable how quickly past injuries were forgotten. Each thought only of himself, and of how he might be reinstated in the good opinion of the now powerful Fox. Swarming up, they showered congratulations on him, all hastening to remind Reynard of their loyalty and friendship. Few cared to notice the defeated Wolf being carried off to have his wounds dressed by the Cat and Bear.

Although delighted at his victory, Reynard had no wish to linger. Bowing low, he thanked his royal benefactor and quickly took his leave.

Reynard went straight home, where he was welcomed most tenderly by Ermelin.

That same evening he sat outside the castle walls watching his cubs play in the fading warmth of the setting sun. He knew how worthless was the flattery of the fickle courtiers, but he knew too, that he had only just escaped with his life, and that from now on it would be wise to mend his ways.

But even as these thoughts were passing through his head, Reynard's ears were pricked, his yellow eyes already fixed on two plump young creatures making their unwary way along the road to Malepardus.

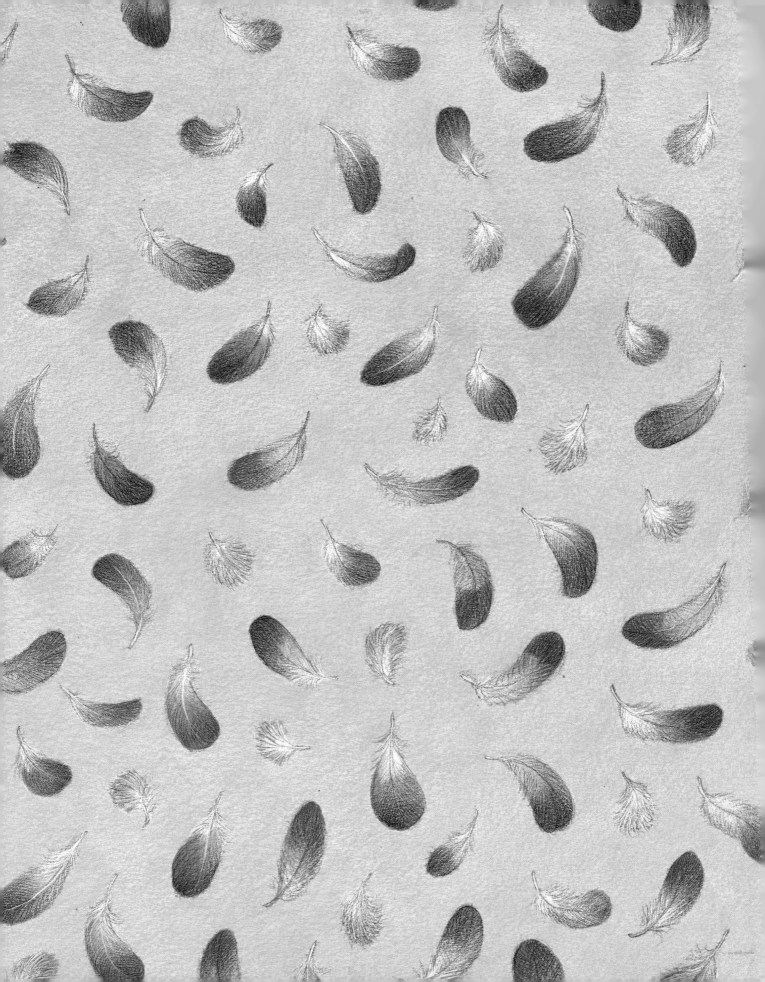